Original title:
The Stillness of Snowflakes

Author: Jameson Hartfield
ISBN HARDBACK: 978-9916-94-544-5
ISBN PAPERBACK: 978-9916-94-545-2

Pastel Parables of Winter

Flakes descend with grace, so light,
Dressing trees in gleaming white.
They skip and dance, a winter show,
Chasing squirrels, moving slow.

A quick spin on a snowy spree,
A snowman grins, just wait and see!
He topples over, laughs galore,
He says, "I can’t take it anymore!"

Nightfall's Gentle Caress

When dark descends, the flakes align,
A soft embrace, oh so divine.
They sneak up quiet, like a thief,
Turning rooftops into a sheaf.

A dog prances, a snowball flies,
He eats it quick, oh what a surprise!
The cat just watches from afar,
Judging antics, like a star.

Stillness Wrapped in White

In the hush, a tiny giggle,
As snowflakes start to wiggle.
They toss and tumble, spin around,
Falling softly, without a sound.

A child's laughter fills the air,
Building castles, unaware.
With every throw, a snowball flies,
Hitting the dad, much to his surprise!

Serene Shades of Winter

In snowy realms, the silence sings,
Sounds muffled by the fluffy wings.
But wait! A flock of ducks appear,
Waddling in boots, oh what a cheer!

They slip and slide on patches slick,
Trying to dance, but what a trick!
As snowmen laugh with noses stout,
Can't they see? The ducks are out!

Floating Dreams on a Chilling Breeze

Fluffy dancers in the air,
Whisper secrets without care.
They twirl and spin, oh what a sight,
In winter's cloak, they bring delight.

A snowman wears a carrot nose,
As flakes tickle and play, who knows?
With frozen giggles and frosty cheer,
They bounce around like frosty deer.

Glistening Feathers of Frost

Chubby flakes with shiny coats,
Drifting down like fluffy boats.
They land on hats, on noses too,
Silly snowflakes, where are you?

A snowball fight begins to brew,
With laughter loud and skies so blue.
They stick to cheeks in giggly glee,
Like icy kisses from the sea.

A Symphony of Frozen Grace

Waltzing down on twinkling toes,
They dance like whispers, no one knows.
In chilly air, they swirl and glide,
Like tiny passengers on a ride.

Joking with the chilly breeze,
They sneak up softly, do as they please.
With each new flake, there’s joy anew,
It’s hard to frown when they come through.

Beneath the Veil of White

Under blankets, all aglow,
Flakes gather round for the winter show.
Tickling noses, they gently fall,
A soft embrace that covers all.

They bring a shimmer, light and bright,
Transforming roads to pure delight.
As laughter fills the frozen air,
Who knew that winter's chill could care?

Quietude Between Blizzards

Flakes dance like gossip at a café,
Whispers tickle, then drift away.
A snowman grins with a carrot nose,
Wondering where the lost mittens go.

Sleds slide by, full of laughter,
Snowball fights lead to playful disaster.
Even the trees wear jackets of white,
Guarding secrets in the soft twilight.

Treading Softly on Flurries

Tiptoe through the fluffy ground,
Each crunch a giggle, a playful sound.
Snowflakes twirl in a chilly waltz,
While penguins ponder if they'll halt.

Frosty footprints line the way,
Leading to trouble at the end of the day.
Snow forts rise like castles grand,
With every throw, we take a stand.

Parchments of Ice

Winter's notebook is filled with fun,
Pages turned when the day is done.
Each flurry writes a story so bright,
Of snowmen battles in pure delight.

Kids armed with snowballs, ready to aim,
A symphony of laughter, a chilly game.
One slip, oh dear! Down they go,
As winter witnesses their funny show.

Murmurs Beneath the Frost

Underneath the icy sheet,
Whispers of snowflakes quietly meet.
Giggles echo through the frozen air,
As snow angels paint without a care.

Hot chocolate spills from chilly hands,
The frosty woods turn to playful lands.
In this realm of winter wonder,
Laughter roars like a thunder.

Time Held in a Frigid Grip

Frosted clocks tick slow, like snails,
Snowmen dance in icy gales.
They sip tea on frozen chairs,
While penguins wear their snazzy wares.

Icicles drip like raucous laughs,
Snowflakes join in winter's gaffs.
Time's forgotten, so they prance,
In the chill, they break their stance.

Soft Kisses from the Sky

Fluffy flakes descend with grace,
A giggle on a chilly face.
They tickle noses, cold and bright,
Creating joy in winter's night.

With cheeks aglow, the snowflakes tease,
Whispers dance upon the breeze.
A soft embrace, oh what a sight,
As winter's hugs bring pure delight.

A Ballet of Winter's Breath

Twirl and spin, the flakes arrive,
In tutus white, they gleefully thrive.
Mice in tuxedos cheer and shout,
What a performance, without a doubt!

With pirouettes in frosty air,
They play tag with an icy flare.
A choreographed, chilly show,
In knees-deep fluff, they leap and flow.

Clouded Secrets Descend

Whispers from clouds, a sneaky plot,
They tumble down, a chilly lot.
Their secrets wrapped in layers bright,
A playful drift - oh, what a sight!

Each flake holds tales of winter's fun,
Of snowball fights and warming sun.
They giggle as they softly land,
With every kiss, they make a band.

Lull of the Frozen Earth

Frosted whispers float around,
Each flake dances, soft and round.
Socks are missing, boots are tight,
Snowmen giggle in pure delight.

Snowball fights bring laughter loud,
While plump penguins form a crowd.
Chill of air makes noses red,
As frosty tales fill up our head.

Silvery Light on Lonesome Paths

Beneath the moon, a rabbit hops,
In winter coats, the clumsy flops.
Sledding down the hill with glee,
The trees whisper jokes, can you hear me?

Puffing clouds like frosty steam,
The snowflakes join in on the dream.
Hot cocoa spills, a marshmallow fight,
We all collapse, what a silly sight!

Winged Dreams of Winter

A snowflake lands upon a nose,
And everyone giggles, goodness knows!
Penguins wander, waddle and play,
While frosty breezes whisk us away.

Icicles hang like silly beards,
As frosty bunnies jester, no fears.
Frosty fingers, red cheeks ablaze,
In this chilly, comical maze!

Spheres of Crystalline Calm

Jolly laughter fills the air,
As snow piles rise without a care.
A snowflake sneezed! Oh, watch it fly,
Into the cup of a startled guy.

Frosty heads in puffy hats,
Chasing tails of playful cats.
Falling softly, like a dream,
Life in winter is quite the scheme!

Shimmering Silence

In a flurry, they take flight,
Twisting, turning, what a sight!
They land like clumsy little stars,
Expecting applause, but just some cars.

Silent giggles in the cold air,
Snowmen frown, they can't compare.
With noses made of carrots bright,
They know they're not quite right!

Frosted Dreams

A snowball flies, it’s pure delight,
But hits a friend, oh what a fright!
They slip and slide on icy bends,
Laughing through each snowy end.

Hot cocoa spills, oh what a waste,
As marshmallows take off in haste.
Chasing fluff like little elves,
Dreaming of warmer, sunlit shelves!

Whispers in the Wind

A gentle flurry tickles my nose,
As snowflakes dance like elegant pros.
“Catch me!” one giggles, “I’m on the run!”
But melts in laughter, oh, what fun!

Friends make angels, oh what a sight,
Flapping wings, not quite right!
With each landing, they create a scene,
That rivals even the best cuisine!

Beneath the Frigid Glow

Under streetlights, they twinkle with glee,
A snowman's hat is a sight to see.
He tips and sways in the chilling breeze,
Forgetting he's melting, oh, what a tease!

Snowball fights turn into slip-ups,
As laughter echoes with joyful hiccups.
Each frosty mishap a comic show,
In the midst of winter's frosty glow!

Frosted Secrets

Little flakes tumble, a clumsy parade,
Whispering secrets in a winter charade.
They land on my nose, a frosty surprise,
Laughing softly, they cover my eyes.

Snowmen grinning with carrot noses,
Slipping and sliding, oh how it dozes!
A snowball fight turns into a mess,
I'm covered in white—oh, what a dress!

When Silence Sings

In a hush, they dance, those cheeky little flakes,
Twirling like ballerinas, for goodness sakes!
They tickle the rooftops and chat with the trees,
While squirrels throw their paws up, “We’re not at ease!”

The ground wears a blanket, cozy and bright,
While penguins in pajamas think it’s just right.
And then comes a dog on a mad winter spree,
Rolling in snow, “Is this blanket for me?”

A Tapestry of Crystal Dreams

Frosty designs that shimmer and play,
Unruly artists with no time to stay.
One dribbles down and lands on my chair,
“Excuse me,” it giggles, “I’m just passing air!”

As I build a castle, oh, what a sight!
The towers are toppling, not holding tight.
“A moat of warm cocoa” I proudly declare,
But the dog jumps in—now it’s everywhere!

Ghosts of the Frozen Sky

Whispering down like a ghostly ballet,
They flutter and twist, making mischief all day.
They gather like gossip through the chilly air,
And I hear them giggle; do they really care?

With a puff, they vanish, a quick little trick,
“Now you see us, now you don’t!”—what a flick!
They pile on my boots, a slippery scheme,
Chasing me home with their crystalline dream!

Hibernation's Lullaby

In blankets deep, I start to snore,
My dreams of warmth, I can't ignore.
The chilly breeze gives me a tease,
As I snooze on with utmost ease.

Each flake that falls, a playful prank,
My coffee's cold, I feel like plank.
The snowmen grin, they steal my hat,
I'll get them back, and that is that!

Snowbound Serenity

Outside it’s white, a frosty prank,
While I stay snug, a cozy tank.
The dog's outside making his mark,
But slips and slides, it’s quite a lark!

The rooftops wear their fluffy crowns,
As squirrels dive, and tumble down.
I sip my cocoa, watch the show,
Winter’s fun, but I’ll never go!

Elegy for a Winter's Night

The evening quiet, sounds of snow,
As I misplace my borrowed glow.
A sock fights hard for its own space,
Lost in the depths of this cold place!

So frosty toes take their own stand,
While ice cubes laugh, placed in my hand.
And from the window, I see, oh dear,
A snowball fight? But I’m not near!

Cascade of White Wishes

A flurry fell, it stole my shoe,
Now both my feet are cold and blue!
The kid next door, with snowball stock,
Goals to pelt me — watch the clock!

He’s building forts, I tip my hat,
While plotting ways to dodge that spat.
With every flake, a whimsy war,
Bring on the fun, let’s snow some more!

Hushed Moments in the Quiet Realm

In a world where silence plays,
Snowflakes dance in silly ways.
Caught mid-air, they toss and twirl,
Making giggles in a whirl.

Fluffy hats for trees they wear,
Tickling noses, everywhere.
With each drop, a playful plop,
Making winter's laughter stop.

Snowball fights where no one wins,
Laughter echoes, cheeky grins.
They fall as if on trampoline,
Bouncing off like a silly scene.

So let them fall, a frosty jest,
Nature's joke, the very best.
In every flake a chuckle lies,
A comedy from cloudy skies.

Each Unique, a Gentle Touch

Sneeze! A flake lands on my nose,
How about that? A frosty pose.
Each one’s face a quirky grin,
I guess that’s how the fun begins.

Kite-like shapes, they swirl around,
Landing softly on the ground.
A unique touch from way up high,
Creating laughter in the sky.

Collect them on a mitten’s fold,
The chilly gems, so brave and bold.
Yet one snowflake sticks in a pout,
It whispers, 'Hey, I’m different, doubt?'

Among the jokes of winter chill,
A gentle humor finds its thrill.
And when they melt, it’s no sad tale,
Just giggles left, like a funny trail.

Lullabies of the Falling Flurry

Whispers soft as silk descend,
In frosty hugs, the world they mend.
Lullabies of chilled delight,
As they playfully kiss the night.

Lights go dim and shadows creep,
Tiny fluffs, they softly leap.
In a hush, they swirl and sigh,
Making snowmen say goodbye.

A frosty giggle shakes a tree,
Watch out now, it’s coming free!
Snowflakes tumble, do a jig,
Each one spins, a tiny wig.

As they settle, dreams unfold,
In chilly tales, we’re never cold.
Come dance with me till morning breaks,
In this world of frozen flakes.

A Tapestry of Frozen Echoes

A tapestry of white delight,
Woven jokes, crisp and bright.
They whisper secrets to the ground,
While giggles echo all around.

Threads of laughter, spun with care,
Each flake’s mischief fills the air.
Some perform, a frosty show,
Ready, set, unfurl and go!

Falling faster than a cat,
No surprises, just a spat.
As snowballs form, they plot and scheme,
Softest pillows? What a dream!

With every flake, a tale is spun,
A frosty prank, a winter fun.
So when they fall, just join the fun,
In a quiet realm, we are all one.

Soft Landing

Flakes tumble down like clumsy fears,
They dance and twirl, creating cheers.
With hats askew and noses bright,
They land on dogs, what a sight!

A snowball flies, it hits with a splat,
Who knew a snowman could wear a hat?
Kids giggle loud, their cheeks are red,
As snowflakes tickle their tiny heads.

Gloves are damp, and socks they squish,
'Who took my boot?' is the whispered wish.
Frosty footsteps, a slippery fate,
Oh, winter fun can be a debate!

But laughter rings as they all fall,
Snowball fights, a joyful brawl.
In this chill, the world looks so bright,
Let’s stomp through snow until the night!

A Quiet Embrace

Flakes sneak in, they tiptoe shy,
Kissing the ground and making pie.
They cuddle close in a fluffy sheet,
Even the squirrels have coldest feet!

Quaint rooftops wear their frosty gowns,
While quiet streets don their white crowns.
Cats peer out with wide-eyed glee,
'Where's my winter nap?' one seems to plea.

Snowmen wobble with carrot nose,
Looking quite silly in their frozen pose.
Snowballs fly, one lands on a head,
'This is for breakfast,' a child said!

Yet as they melt, they cause a scene,
Puddles gather, a shimmering sheen.
Together we laugh, despite the cold,
Winter's story is fun to be told!

Winter's Gentle Touch

Whispers of white descend like pranksters,
Frosty fingers dance on shrieking pansters.
Children leap with joyful yells,
As snowflakes twirl like tiny bells.

Hot cocoa waits with marshmallows bold,
A warm embrace against winter's cold.
Sipping slow, the laughter's loud,
As rain fills the air with a fluffy cloud.

Snowflakes fall with a giggly thud,
On unsuspecting cars parked in the bud.
Slippery sidewalks become a show,
As skaters glide with much flair and flow.

With cheeks glowing, they make a cheer,
For every frosty moment, winter is dear.
In this waltz of white, we find our grace,
Snowflakes chuckle, oh what a place!

Choreography of Cold

A ballet of flakes pirouettes and twirls,
As children erupt in giggles and swirls.
Chubby mittens build castles of snow,
In this frosty play, time seems slow.

A toddler zooms down a hill with a grin,
'Woohoo!' he shouts, 'Let the fun begin!'
Cousins collide, their laughter bright,
As snowballs bounce like balloons in flight.

Grandpa slips, a comical sight,
Flailing arms in a frosty plight.
His hat flies high, landing on the tree,
While all the kids shout, 'That's so funny!'

As winter ends, the snow fades away,
But memories linger, in a bright array.
In frozen joy, we all have a blast,
Thanks to the cold, winter's spell is cast!

Sighs of a Snowy Dawn

Tiny flakes dance from the sky,
One hits my nose, oh me, oh my!
They swirl and twirl like dizzy bees,
While I just sneeze and clutch my knees.

My hat's a tent, my gloves a joke,
As snowballs fly, I start to choke.
I build a fort, it leans to one side,
A masterpiece where snowflakes hide!

The cold creeps in, my toes are numb,
I scream for tea, my winter fun!
Yet snowmen grin with carrot eyes,
While I slip down—it's no surprise.

The yard's a canvas, pure and white,
I leave my mark, a funny sight!
Children giggle, their laughter rings,
As snowflakes fall on all our things.

Luminance of Borrowed Dreams

Dressed in fluff, a frosty grin,
On my face, the snowflakes spin.
They tickle cheeks and greet the ground,
While I trip over, feet unbound.

Snowball fights and laughter burst,
I dodge and weave, but still get cursed.
One sneaky flank from little Fred,
I never knew that snow could spread!

A snowman talks with a carrot hat,
His icy wisdom—where's it at?
He tips and wobbles, too much cheer,
I think I'll leave him—this is queer.

The world turns bright with frosty flair,
I'm buried deep in jamboree flair.
And in this chill of winter's jest,
I laugh and play—who needs a rest?

Threads of Icy Silence

A whisper drifts through chilly air,
As snowflakes land without a care.
I step outside, oh what a sight,
A winter wonder, pure delight!

My boots are stuck—what needs to budge?
I might be frozen, who can judge?
A snowball rolls, I duck and swerve,
This fight with frost, I must preserve!

With friends we roll a giant ball,
It wobbles much—we're at a stall.
A nose of carrot, limbs of twigs,
A lopsided friend, he's got some digs!

The quiet hush is loud with cheer,
In flurries of laughter, winter's near.
But as I slip on ice today,
I laugh it off, come what may!

Frosted Vignettes

Flakes dance like clumsy ballet,
Twirl on their way to the ground's play.
They giggle and tumble, what a sight,
Coating the world in frosty white.

Hot cocoa in hand, we cheer,
As the flakes stick without a fear.
Snowmen start to form with a grin,
Wearing our scarves, it’s quite the win!

Each flake's a tiny whispered joke,
Wigs of snow on each tree cloak.
Laughter erupts with a chilly breeze,
As we dodging snowballs, feel such ease.

But when they melt, oh what a shame,
Soggy socks are part of the game.
Yet we'll laugh again when they return,
For winter’s a time for us to learn!

Celestial Designs of Stillness

Look out the window, what a show,
Tiny artists in a flurry flow.
They're crafting their art with no one to spy,
Each flake a secret that floats from the sky.

In hats and boots, we slip and slide,
We tumble and fumble, it’s a wild ride.
Giggles erupt from a faceplant's fate,
Winter fun served up on a snow plate.

Snowball fights that bring me glee,
Missed my mark, hit a tree!
Forests giggle, branches creak,
Nature’s laughter, it's all so unique.

When the sun shines what a big tease,
Watch them disappear, with such ease.
Yet the memories of bumbles will stay,
Our snowy humor comes out to play!

Silent Echoes

Footsteps muffled in the white fluff,
Around each corner, the fun is tough.
We trudge along, feeling quite bold,
But a slip makes the chill more cold.

Snowflakes tickle as they drift down,
I trip on the path, and I wear a frown.
But look! There’s a squirrel in a coat,
Dashing around like a fluffy little goat!

Snowy hats fall from our heads,
As we make snow angels in our beds.
Feathers of winter whisper in jest,
For who knew that snow could be a quest?

Now winter's a stage, where laughter grows,
With each chilly adventure that nobody knows.
And when spring arrives with a warm kiss,
We’ll tell tales of snow, and reminisce!

The Gentle Fall

Whirling in chaos, what a delight,
These frozen dancers in soft light.
They flutter about like they own the place,
Landing on noses with comical grace.

Frosty powder on my cheek,
Out in the cold, laughs never meek.
Though shoveling snow is quite the chore,
We trade gloves and giggles, who could want more?

Each landing flake leaves a surprise,
Like tiny fairies with endless pies.
Baking in snow, the cookies take flight,
With frost on our heads, how absurd is that sight?

So snow, come again, we plead in song,
Your antics keep winter lively and strong.
Though we might grumble as we shovel away,
You bring the joy that we can't help but say!

Serenity in Sled Tracks

In a world dressed in white,
Laughter flies like a kite,
Sleds race down with a cheer,
Snowmen grinning ear to ear.

Hot cocoa spills on my coat,
The dog steals my warmest boat,
Snowflakes dance in the air,
While I trip on a snow bear.

Footprints lead to mischief,
As we giggle, feeling stiff,
Frosty noses, cheeks aglow,
Wishing for a sledding show.

But on this snowy spree,
I lost a mitt, oh woe is me!
Joyful chaos, pure delight,
In the calm of winter's white.

Flurry of Tranquility

A blizzard plays peek-a-boo,
With hats and gloves, a wacky crew,
Snowflakes swirl, a fluffy dance,
While I try to retain my pants.

We build a fort, it’s very grand,
Snowball fights with mistletoe bands,
Hot drinks freeze in my cold hands,
But laughter warms these winter lands.

Biting winds, we squeal and run,
Chasing shadows, oh what fun,
As nature laughs, there's not a care,
Except for frostbite, just beware!

In a snow globe world so bright,
Not a single snowman upright,
In the flurry, joy is found,
Winter’s whimsy all around.

Glimmering Silence

A hush falls soft upon the ground,
As little flakes just drift around,
They seem to tumble, swirl and swerve,
With giggles hidden in each curve.

I slip and slide, my balance fails,
While visions of snow-muffled trails,
Mittens clash with my hot drink,
I'm now a snowball, what do you think?

In this quiet, laughter erupts,
As friends throw flakes, we giggle, sup,
Hot pies glide by on a sled-sled race,
Yet it's my warm face that takes first place.

In this shining, chilly spree,
Every bump gives glee to me,
Oh, winter's fun, left and right,
With glimmering silence, all feels right.

Echoes in the Snow

Down the hill, my laughter rolls,
A snow angel's grin quickly grows,
The echo of our joyful screams,
Turns winter days into warm dreams.

We make a snow boss, tall and wide,
With a carrot nose and beady eyes,
He sits there with a frosty glare,
As we chuckle, unaware of care.

Snowflakes whisper secrets near,
As we dodge the cold with cheer,
Sliding faces, and wintery flips,
With icicles that mock our quips.

In this realm of white delight,
We stack our hopes in snowy height,
As echoes of our joy resound,
In frosty joy, our lives are found.

Dandelion Wishes in Frost

A frosty dance, they twirl and spin,
Each flake whispers, "Let the fun begin!"
Like tiny dancers from the sky,
They make me laugh as they drift by.

One lands on my nose, a frosty cheer,
I sneeze and giggle, oh dear, oh dear!
A flurry's coming, I can see,
It's nature's way of tickling me!

Winter's Veil of Tranquility

In the hush of white, a soft surprise,
Snowflakes glide down, oh how they rise!
The world is covered in a frozen quilt,
With laughter shared, the air is spilt.

I caught one on my tongue, what a treat!
Tastes like winter, a lick of sweet!
They tumble down without a care,
In the icy air, we play and share.

Subtle Patterns of the Falling

Little artists in the air,
Painting chaos everywhere!
A snowflake lands with a gentle plop,
And on my head, I feel a drop!

We giggle as we run and slide,
In this white wonderland, we confide.
With every flake, a chuckle bursts,
A winter’s joke, who’d have guessed first?

Reverie in the Frozen Quiet

In this hush, the world holds breath,
Flakes play tag, a dance of death.
No one can see where they've been,
A game of hide and seek they win!

I slip and slide, a comic show,
These snowflakes laugh, "Hey, look at Joe!"
With every fall, a silly fool,
In winter's court, I'm but a tool!

Frosty Allegro

In winter's waltz, they twirl and spin,
Dropping down, they have such a grin,
Like tiny dancers in cozy attire,
They tickle our noses, oh what a choir!

Chasing each other, they tumble and sway,
Landing on rooftops, they'd love to play,
But a gust of wind makes them fly a bit,
Oops! Now they're landing in grandma's mitt!

A grand parade, all fluffy and bright,
They land on snowmen, what a delight!
With carrot noses and hats askew,
These flurries think they're artists too!

Whispers of laughter, a snowball fight,
Boundless joy in the pale moonlight,
Each fall is a giggle, a cheeky delight,
As they rest on our sidewalks, all soft and white!

The Art of Falling Lightly

With grace, they drop, these fluffy folks,
In the air, they’re dodging some jokes,
An aerial ballet that’s all quite absurd,
They catch on to hair, oh, isn’t that stirred?

Glancing down, they see folks rush,
Avoiding the bumps, creating a hush,
They plop on benches, ice-cold delight,
Unicycling squirrels wish they had flight!

Each one's a marvel, unique in design,
They land on my nose; that feels just fine,
Wiggle and jiggle, they bounce all around,
'Til I'm sneezing loudly, and laughing is found!

When they gather in mounds that appear,
Snowball artillery forms over here,
Laughter erupts as a flurry turns,
Into the best winter antics we yearn!

Glacial Embrace

Fluffy friends drifting from skies so high,
Landing with grace, not a single goodbye,
They hug the ground, cozy and light,
In a world turned soft, oh what a sight!

While elves are whispering secrets up there,
These snowflakes chuckle and dance without care,
On rooftops they gather, all fluffy and proud,
Composing a quilt over every frosty shroud.

They play peek-a-boo, then strike silly poses,
Each one a joke, with giggles that closes,
A heavy snowfall turns stripes into waves,
While we slip and slide, oh the fun it saves!

Laughter erupts from slips in the snow,
While snowflakes wink, “This is how we glow!”
Under streetlamps, they twinkle and tease,
Falling on mittens, and tickling our knees!

Footprints in the Soft White

Shimmering paths where shadows dance,
Snowflakes conspire to take their chance,
They sip from our cocoa, oh, isn’t that grand,
As snowmen listen and lend them a hand!

In the chaos of winter, they've gathered in teams,
Plotting to slide down on whimsical dreams,
Footprints abound in this white-coated fun,
As we all tumble down and make a run!

With giggles and joy, they land by the lot,
Flip-flop in the snow, oh the lessons are taught,
Time flies like snowflakes in soft, swirling flight,
As we trip and we fall, all filled with delight!

So here’s to the flurries, with make-believe names,
Playing hopscotch in ice, never winning their games,
They softly remind us, in each frosty flight,
Life is just better when you laugh at the light!

Whispers Through the Winter Light

When flakes begin their dance, so spry,
They tumble down, a clumsy high.
Each one screams, "Catch me if you can!"
But land right there, where not you plan.

A snowball fight breaks out, oh dear!
With snowmen made of cheer and beer.
They melt away, just like my dreams,
Oh winter, how you steal my gleams!

The world is wrapped in white so bright,
Yet children slip with pure delight.
They pretend to fly, arms wide and glee,
While squirrels laugh up in their tree.

So let the flakes come tumbling down,
In winter's joke, we wear a crown.
With icy smiles and frozen toes,
We live for laughs as winter slows.

A Blanket of Silent Teardrops

There’s laughter whispered on the breeze,
As snowflakes drift like sneezy peas.
A frozen slip upon the walk,
Looks like a snowman’s wannabe talk.

Why do these flakes come down to play?
They spread their chill in such a way.
Each landing flap, a comic fail,
Our winter antics tell the tale.

Around the streets, like kittens prance,
Chasing a swirl in a silly dance.
Each murmur of joy speaks, "Oh my,"
As sleds zoom by, we're flying high!

So toast to flakes that fall from grace,
In winter’s waltz, we find our place.
With cups of cocoa, let’s unite,
In laughter pure, we’ll brave the night.

Gathering Where Silence Sings

In parks where quiet claims the night,
Snowflakes fall like confetti light.
They giggle down with all their might,
And land to play in cozy white.

Each flake is unique, or so they say,
Yet they all just want to have a play.
They land on hats, on noses too,
And giggle best when they hit a shoe.

A snowman blushes with a carrot nose,
While everyone giggles and carefully toes.
Riding hills with laughter loud,
Their frosty faces feel so proud.

So raise your cups to winter's charm,
Where it’s too easy to spread the warm.
Though the cold comes rushing in,
Our hearts are full, and that’s our win.

The Elegance of Frozen Air

Oh how they tumble, white and bold,
Each crystal's tale is yet untold.
With every gust, they whirl about,
Creating chaos, hop and shout.

Elf-like giggles ride the air,
While icicles form with utmost flair.
Watch out now, another flake will fall!
A conga line on a trampoline wall.

Kids with cheeks all rosy red,
Waddle like penguins, no fear ahead.
They trip and slide, then laugh and cheer,
"More snowflakes, please, let's disappear!"

So in this season, let's all sing,
And sway with glee, let laughter ring.
Though fingers freeze and noses run,
In winter's world, we dance for fun!

Underneath the Quiet Sky

Frosty whispers dance in the air,
As snowflakes tumble with little care.
They tickle your nose and stick to your shoe,
"Is that a flake or a bird?" I asked the crew.

Laughter erupts with each chilly drift,
Bumbling around in this wintry gift.
Each flake a comedian, falling with grace,
They slip through the air, like popcorn in space.

When bundled up tightly, I can’t find my hat,
Oh wait, it’s right here! On a snowman’s flat!
The snowmen are grinning, looking quite spry,
Wishing for mittens, they wave with a sigh.

Embraced by Influence

Snowflakes take turns, a parade on the street,
Like little wise minions, they share their retreat.
One knocks on my window, all sparkly and bright,
"I'm here for a visit, to bring you delight!"

Slipping and sliding, in total disarray,
They tickle the pavement, as people just sway.
With each little laugh, they gather on toes,
"Look at me! I'm a flake!" then down they go!

Cocoa in hand, we all take a pause,
Flakes down below cause a laughter-filled cause.
With sugar and cream, it's a heavenly mix,
But snowflakes find ways to cause silly tricks.

Petals of Ice

Petals of ice drift down from the sky,
I chased a few fancies that twirled right by.
They whispered in glee, "Catch me if you dare!"
But I just tripped over a frozen old chair.

Each flake a dancer, with lessons to share,
"Fall gracefully now!" said one with a flair.
With bellyflops landing, they giggled in flight,
'Till the ground caught my feet and put up a fight.

In a flurry, we twirled under clouds full of dreams,
The snowflakes all grinned at my flopping schemes.
“Next time take your time!” they flitted with zest,
And sprinkled their laughter, a snow-covered jest.

The Poetry of Chill

Chilled little whispers in the morning light,
Snowflakes rehearsing their graceful delight.
They giggle and quibble, as they dodge and weave,
Doing the tango, while we take our leave.

With hats on our heads and scarves wrapped so tight,
They tease from above, "Come join in our flight!"
We slip on the ice, they shower us with cheer,
"Admit it," they laugh, "We taught you that fear!"

In blankets of white, their little hearts glow,
They dote on the children who play in the snow.
A chorus of chill with a jolly refrain,
We dance through the flurries—oh, what a campaign!

Chasing Shadows of a Feathered Night

Up in the sky, a fowl took flight,
With flapping wings that caused delight.
It swooped and dove through moonlit beams,
While chasing shadows in its dreams.

But as it danced on fluffy snow,
It slipped and slid - oh, what a show!
It flopped and tumbled, wings askew,
While giggles echoed, who knew it too?

A squirrel watched from his frosty nook,
In stitches, he read the scene like a book.
He chortled loud, then hid from sight,
As the bird kept failing on its flight.

Oh, feathered night, so full of fun,
Your clumsy moves; you're number one!
We'll raise a toast to your snowy spree,
With laughter that lasts – it's pure glee!

The Poetry of Winter's Touch

A snowflake fell with quite a flair,
It twinkled down without a care.
It tickled noses, stole some hats,
And wandered off to tease the cats.

They swatted wildly, missed it so,
As it pirouetted to and fro.
It danced atop a frozen brook,
Then snuck beneath a snugged-up nook.

Oh winter’s charm, in sly disguise,
Turns icy air to sweet surprise.
Where giggles echo, hearts take flight,
In every flake, there’s pure delight.

So here’s to frolics in the snow,
A world of wonder, steal the show!
Each flake a jest, a playful touch,
In winter’s realm that we love so much!

Whispers of Winter

A gentle hush, the world in white,
But little critters dance in delight.
The rabbit bounces, the badger winks,
As winter chuckles and quietly blinks.

Snowballs fly, with laughter loud,
Creating chaos – so proud, so proud!
The whispers turn to roars of glee,
In frosty realms where all are free.

The owls hoot softly, wise and sly,
As snowflakes swirl and cheekily fly.
They giggle and flap, in the chilly space,
"We're here for the fun, not just to grace!"

So let the winter's whispers play,
With creatures bold who laugh all day.
Each wobbly step on the icy ground,
Brings joy and mirth all around!

Dance of Silent Feathers

A feather floated, soft and light,
And landed on a pup's delight.
He sprang in place, a doggy dancer,
And twirled around, the feather's prancer.

It slipped and flopped, much to his chase,
Around the yard, it found its space.
The pup barked loud, a playful game,
While neighbors smiled at such a claim.

Oh, to behold this snowy sight,
Where laughter twirls in purest light!
A blizzard's joke, a feather's prank,
As winter giggles in the bank.

So let them frolic, let them sway,
The laughter echoes all the day.
With dancing pups and flying cheer,
In feathered fun we long to hear!

Solitude in Chills

A snowflake lands on my nose,
It giggles as it quickly froze.
I dance around in winter's breeze,
While snowmen laugh, saying, "Please!"

The chilly air, so crisp and bright,
Makes squirrels wear a jacket tight.
I slip and slide on icy trails,
While penguins waddle with their snails.

A frosty world of white delight,
Where snowballs soar, oh what a sight!
I shout and cheer, then trudge back home,
To sip on cocoa, blissfully roam.

So here I sit, all snug and warm,
With winter's chill, I find my charm.
The snowflakes swirl, a goofy crew,
Just waiting for more fun to ensue!

Cascades of Calm

A flurry starts, the rooftops gleam,
A snowball fight? Oh, what a dream!
The flakes are festive, in their play,
They tickle noses along the way.

Chilly giggles fill the air,
As fluffy ghosts float everywhere.
Some hop like bunnies, some roll like logs,
Creating chaos, those silly clogs!

A snowman wears my dad’s old hat,
And waves to birds who shout, 'Just chat!'
The trees are dressed in coats so bright,
While I make snow angels in delight.

The laughter rings, a joyful cheer,
In this white wonderland, we steer.
Wouldn't trading toes for warmth be grand?
Yet I still stomp in this snowy land!

Hushed Hearts of Frost

In the silence, snowflakes joke,
They tumble down with playful poke.
With each soft thud upon my head,
I grin and hear their laughter spread.

My boots are lost, submerged in white,
The flakes conspire in sheer delight.
They race ahead, I trail behind,
With snowy giggles, oh so kind.

A frosty breeze, a chilly sigh,
My cheeks so red, I can't deny!
The world’s a canvas, blank and fun,
Yet chilly noses like frozen buns!

Each snowflake plays its quirky role,
As I start losing all control.
I trip and fall in this winter play,
With laughter echoing all the way!

Veils of White

A blanket thick, so soft and bright,
Unruly snowflakes cause a fright.
They tumble down like mischief's swarm,
In chaos wrapped, they tease the warm.

My gloves are stuck to my cold hands,
While reindeer dance in snowy bands.
The winter air, a frosty cheer,
As everyone manages to veer!

Each flake unique, a dizzy spin,
They tickle cheeks as I begin.
I toss and twirl in this white sea,
And laugh at my plight—just let me be!

Frosty friends, they join the fun,
Creating whirlwinds, on the run.
And here we laugh in icy glee,
These silly flakes, so wild and free!

Glassy Webs of Winter

Tiny dancers twirl and sway,
Kittens think it's time to play.
They leap and pounce, then slip and slide,
In icy threads, they take a ride.

Frosty curls upon their paws,
Making feline acrobats pause.
With every twist, they sport a grin,
Chasing flakes like they're a win.

Snowmen's noses made of coal,
Watch the chaos take its toll.
Wobbly builds go down with glee,
As giggling kids shout "Look at me!"

Flakes fall gently, soft and light,
Creating laughter, pure delight.
While sleds fly by in blissful haste,
Leaving behind a snowy waist.

Winter whispers with a jest,
As snowflakes put our skills to test.
Falling softly, laughter spreads,
While icy pranks fill all our heads.

Celestial Drift

Silly realms of frosted bliss,
Flakes dance down with a snowman's kiss.
They float like feathers, soft and slow,
But watch out—here comes a slippery show!

Children's laughter fills the air,
As snowballs join the playful scare.
Aiming high, then splat they fly,
Who needs to aim? Oh me, oh my!

Up above, the clouds conspire,
Meeting ground with mischief, they retire.
Whirling in whimsical delight,
Snow angels giggle through the night.

To catch one, we'll leap and dive,
Rolling, tumbling—oh, how we thrive!
In these frozen waltzes, oh so bold,
The prankster's tale of winter told.

Muffled Elegance

Whispers fall, like secrets shared,
As snowflakes drift, slightly impaired.
Bounding along in soft delight,
Unruly shapes in pure white light.

Wearing hats made of frosty lace,
They tumble down without a trace.
Puppies leap and give a bark,
Trying to catch that icy spark.

All dressed up in nature's quilt,
Making fun of how they wilt.
But noble mounds stand proud and tall,
Ready for kids to take a fall!

Here comes a joyful, snowy cheer,
As laughter echoes far and near.
In floppy boots, on slippery ground,
We're all winners when snow is found.

A Mosaic of Quietude

Patterns fall like silly jokes,
A white parade with quirky folks.
Muffled giggles in drifting air,
As snowflakes land without a care.

Snowball fights erupt with flair,
While sledding kids ignite the stare.
With rosy cheeks, they spin and twirl,
In this glorious winter whirl.

Twirling glimmers, frosty gems,
Caught in giggles, like little hems.
A snowman sports a hat too large,
While winter whispers, “Here’s the charge!”

And still they fall, like cheeky sprites,
Joining hands in playful fights.
A mosaic of messy fun,
Our chilly laughter—never done.

Reflections in Snowy Murmurs

Fluffy bits dance down from above,
Falling softly like a dove.
I slip and slide on a winter's prank,
With laughter echoing from the bank.

A snowball flies, a cheeky grin,
I'm caught off guard, let the games begin!
With each frosty flurry, mischief brews,
As cold toes threaten my cheerful shoes.

Icicles dangle like crooked teeth,
I wonder if they ever greet.
With chilly whispers tickling my ear,
I giggle, then tumble—oh dear, oh dear!

While snowflakes giggle in silent glee,
They plot and scheme, oh wily spree!
In this winter wonder, we all collide,
Joyful chaos in the snowy tide.

Frosted Vows

Under frosted roofs, we scribble hearts,
Making promises with chilly parts.
But snowballs fly, and vows get lost,
As laughter erupts, it's worth the cost!

With rosy cheeks and frosty bites,
Bundled in layers, we scale new heights.
Flakes swirl around, a clumsy dance,
Amidst our twirls, who needs romance?

We pledge to stay warm, to never freeze,
But each snowman becomes a tease.
With carrot noses and silly hats,
Our frozen friends engage in chats!

So here's to winter's funny show,
Where laughter and snowflakes freely flow.
Through icy winds, our spirits soar,
With frosted vows, who could ask for more?

Twinkling Overhead

Stars twinkle brightly in the night,
But snowflakes sparkle, oh what a sight!
They fall like hopes, each unique grace,
Creating a winter wonderland embrace.

As I catch one on my tongue, oh bliss,
A chilly treat I cannot miss!
But wait! What's this? A snowflake's sneeze?
I laugh aloud, frozen in the breeze!

A blizzard twirls, painting the town,
With snowy brushstrokes, none wear a frown.
From rooftops high, the flakes do glide,
Frosty giggles as we all take a ride!

With snowmen grinning, we skate and spin,
Creating snowy chaos, let the fun begin!
Beneath twinkling lights, and frosty dreams,
We dance with flurries, bursting at the seams!

A Symphony of White

A symphony starts with a chilly sigh,
As flakes fall down from the silvery sky.
They twirl and glide with a whimsical charm,
In this frosty orchestra, we'd do no harm.

Snowflakes shimmy, like dancers so spry,
Conducting their numbers, oh me, oh my!
With flurries of laughter, and chilly notes,
We chase after them as our joy floats.

In this winter concert, I've lost my hat,
While a snowman beams, looking quite fat.
With jingle bells ringing, we sing out loud,
Creating a ruckus, a jubilant crowd!

So let’s play a tune on this snowy stage,
With every giggle, we turn a new page.
In this symphony of white, let’s cherish the fun,
For winter’s our concert, and we’re not yet done!

Prism of Snow-Kissed Silence

Flakes in a dance, all spin and swirl,
Frosty confetti starts to unfurl.
They tickle my nose and nest in my hair,
Unsuspecting guests who catch me unaware.

Snowman grins wide, with a carrot for a nose,
He seems to know secrets, but never shows.
Round and jolly, he sways in delight,
Until the sun comes, and he takes his flight!

Laughter erupts when I slip on the ice,
A winter ballet that isn't so nice.
Neighbors all chuckle as I tumble and roll,
A snow-covered critter has claimed my sole goal!

The quiet is lively, the night cannot sleep,
As monster snowflakes in rhythm, they leap.
With giggles and frost, they play a quick game,
Leaving us laughing, yet never the same.

Ethereal Winter Waltz

Twinkling flakes fall like ballerinas,
Waltzing through air with dazzling vistas.
They tiptoe on rooftops, a dazzling sight,
As I sip on cocoa, it feels quite right!

Dancing with snowmen, oh what a sight,
Their noses all crooked, they bring such delight.
We spin and we twirl, till the sun comes in,
Then our frozen waltz ends with a goofy grin!

Snowball fights erupt with playful cheers,
As snowflakes giggle and melt all our fears.
But wait! Here comes Fido, a wild little chap,
He leaps and he bounds, giving snowflakes a slap!

Chirps from the birds make a merry refrain,
As snowflakes start singing, the joy’s never plain.
We dance with the chill, let the giggling flow,
In a world made of laughter, where snowmen do glow!

Liquid Moonlight on Snow

Moonlit flurries glide on a silver stream,
Snowball fights start, like a whimsical dream.
Each flake a giggle, each crunch a delight,
As we tumble and roll through the crisp, cold night.

With socks on my hands, I sift through the chill,
Building a fortress, my own frosty hill.
But the puppy has come, with a wag and a bite,
He thinks that my castle is his new delight!

The moon shines above, with a cheeky grin,
It snickers and giggles as snowflakes dive in.
With whispers of play, the night starts to glow,
While we chuckle and tumble in soft, powdery snow.

Laughter so bright in the shimmering light,
Snowflakes now dance with an air of delight.
Our fun flows like rivers, round corners it bends,
In this liquid moonlight, where mischief transcends!

Tranquility’s Blanket

A gentle hush falls like a sleepy quilt,
While snowflakes giggle, their mischief is built.
They blanket the world with a soft, frosty cheer,
As I trip on my laces—I just can't steer!

Wading through powder, I chime with glee,
As my neighbors cheer, 'Look! It's so free!'
They toss snowballs, but they miss, oh dear,
And instead, hit Old Man Jenkins who’s near!

Now he’s grumpy with a snow-covered hat,
His beard all white-powdered, he looks like a cat.
But soon he’s laughing, joining in too,
As winter ignites a jolly crew.

And beneath all that laughter, we find a repose,
In the snuggly calm where the chilly wind blows.
With giggles surrounding, this season does sing,
Wrapped up in a blanket, where troubles take wing!

Choreography of Ghostly Beauty

Fluffy dancers drift from the sky,
Twirling softly, oh my, oh my!
They land in a heap, slightly askew,
Making my mittens look like a zoo.

A waltz of white on the street they prance,
Each twist and twirl is a snowy romance.
I stumble and slip, my cheeks turning red,
As they giggle and tease, jump right on my head.

A soft serenade for the squirrels that peek,
While I flail like a yeti, so goofy and weak.
They laugh as I tumble, all frosty and bright,
In the dance of the flakes, I've lost all my might.

So here in the chaos, let laughter unfold,
For winter's a show that never gets old.
As flakes take their bow, I can’t help but grin,
In the choreography of beauty, let’s all join in!

The Art of White Silence

In quiet moments, oh what a sight,
A carpet of wonders that gleams in the night.
But watch where you step, it’s a sneaky affair,
One slip of the foot, and you’re caught in mid-air.

All snowflakes come down with a giggle and cheer,
Creating a world where we freeze up with fear.
With tongues out to catch, we’re kids once again,
And our laughter erupts like it’s snowing, amen!

Each flake whispers tales that only they know,
Of mischief and giggles in the warmth of the glow.
They tickle your nose, and they tease at your toes,
In the art of silence, we forget all our woes.

So let’s savor this hush, as the world twirls around,
With snowflakes composing the softest of sounds.
In the canvas of white, we’ll chuckle and play,
As the art of the moment melts worries away.

Magic in Every Delicate Drift

Softly they flutter, like whispers in flight,
Each flake carries secrets from day into night.
Dancing like fairies, they spin through the air,
While I trip on their magic, with style and flair.

They gather in corners, those cheeky little sprites,
Hiding beneath bushes, keeping warm through the nights.
With a chuckle, they blanket the world in their glee,
But watch out, dear friend; they're all watching me!

With laughter and joy, they slip by your nose,
But it's a snowball that lands—oh, where did it go?
In a shower of giggles, we tumble and roll,
Finding magic in drifts and a bright merry soul.

So let's celebrate flurries as they tickle our toes,
In the whimsy of winter, let hilarity flow.
For in every soft snowfall, there's wonder to see,
As we revel in magic, together, you and me!

Emptiness Painted in Snow

A blank canvas sprawls, oh what a delight,
With brushstrokes of white, the world feels polite.
But underneath that softness lies mischief and fun,
As snowmen plot schemes beneath the bright sun.

Look closely to find, in this frosty expanse,
Squirrel mischief-makers do a good little dance.
While penguins in hats sing a curious tune,
And all of our worries get lost in the swoon.

Yet here I must tell, with a laughter-filled sigh,
Even a snowball might just catch you awry.
With a plop and a splat, my plans swiftly blow,
As I face the great winter, all painted in snow.

So let's raise our mittens and cherish the chill,
For emptiness holds all the joy we can fill.
In a swirling white wonder, together we'll play,
In a laughter-filled world where snow doesn't stay!

Milton Keynes UK
Ingram Content Group UK Ltd.
UKHW020817141124
451205UK00012B/619

9 789916 945452